now you're cookin'
CURRIES

© 2007 Rebo International b.v., Lisse, The Netherlands

This title is a revision of title Curries that was published by Rebo Productions in 1997.

Original recipes and photos: Rolli Books

Design and layout: Minkowsky Graphics, Enkhuizen, The Netherlands

Typesetting: AdAm Studio, Prague, The Czech Republic

Cover design: Minkowsky Graphics, Enkhuizen, The Netherlands

Proofreading: Sarah Dunham

ISBN: 978-90-366-2239-4

now you're cookin'
CURRIES

THIS BOOK JUST MAKES YOU WANNA COOK

REBO PUBLISHERS

Not all curries are spicy. In this book, we offer a collection of recipes that vary in character from the mildly aromatic and rich and creamy to the pungently spiced and fiery hot. Any one of the hotter curries can be made milder by simply reducing the amount of chillies used.

Basic Curry Recipes

Paneer

In a saucepan, bring 3 quarts of milk to a boil. Just before the milk boils, add 6 tbsp of lemon juice or vinegar to curdle the milk. Strain the curdled milk through a piece of muslin to allow all the whey and moisture to drain away. Still wrapped in the muslin, place the paneer under a weight and refrigerate for 2-3 hours to allow it to set into a block. The paneer can then be cut or grated from the block.

Garlic paste and ginger paste

Soak 10 ½ oz of fresh ginger or garlic cloves overnight to soften the skins. Peel and chop roughly. Process in a food processor, or pound with a pestle and mortar, until pulped. The pulp can be stored in an airtight container and refrigerated for 4–6 weeks.

Onion paste

Peel and chop 1 lb 2 oz onions into quarters. Process in a food processor, or pound with a pestle and mortar, until pulped. Refrigerate in an airtight container for 4–6 weeks.

Cashew nut and almond paste

Process 10 ½ oz of blanched almonds or raw cashew nuts in a food processor, or pound with a pestle and mortar, with enough peanut or vegetable oil to form a thick paste. Process or pound until fairly smooth. Refrigerate in an airtight container.

Green chilli or red chilli paste

Roughly chop the required amount of green or red chillies, and process in a food processor, or pound with a pestle and mortar, until pulped.

Coconut paste

Crack open a fresh coconut, reserving the coconut milk, and break in half. Carefully remove the coconut flesh from the hard shell with a knife and break into 1-in pieces. Process in a food processor with a little coconut milk, or pound with a pestle and mortar, until pulped.

Poppy seed paste

Process poppy seeds in a food processor, or pound with a pestle and mortar, with enough vegetable oil to form a paste.

Garam masala

Garam masala is widely available as a ready-prepared spice mix, but it is easy to make your own mix and is likely to be fresher and more aromatic than the shop-bought variety.

Finely grind together the following ingredients: 3 ¼ oz cumin seeds, 2 ½ oz black peppercorns, 2 ¾ oz black cardamom seeds, 1 oz fennel seeds, 1 ½ oz green cardamoms, 1 ¼ oz coriander seeds, ¾ oz cloves, 20 cinnamon sticks, 1 in in length, ¾ oz ground mace, ¾ oz black cumin seeds, ½ oz dried rose petals, ½ oz dried bay leaves, ½ oz ground ginger. Store in an airtight container in a cool, dry place.

Method

Cut the chicken into bite-sized pieces. Soak the saffron in a little water in a small bowl for 10 minutes. Drain and set aside. Meanwhile, heat the oil in a saucepan and add the chopped garlic. Cook until brown. Add the onions and cook until slightly browned, stirring occasionally. Add the cinnamon, cloves and cardamoms and cook until the onions turn golden brown. Add the ginger and garlic pastes, chicken, salt and yellow or red chilli powder. Stir for 3–4 minutes. Add the chicken stock and bring to a boil. Cover and simmer for about 30 minutes or until the chicken is cooked and tender. Remove the pan from the heat. Remove the chicken using a slotted spoon and keep hot. Strain the juices, discarding any pulp. Return the juices to the pan, bring to a boil and boil rapidly until the sauce is thickened and reduced. Add the chicken and reheat thoroughly. Stir in the prepared saffron and serve.

Ingredients

1 lb 12 oz boneless chicken thighs

A pinch of saffron

5 tbsp vegetable oil

1 oz garlic, chopped

2 small onions, sliced

1-inch piece of cinnamon stick

10 cloves

4 cardamoms

Pot Cooked Chicken

4 tsp ginger paste (page 4)

4 tsp garlic paste (page 4)

Salt, to taste

½ tsp yellow or red chilli powder

2 ¼ cups chicken stock

Variation

Use half white or red wine and half stock in place of all stock, for a richer flavor.

chicken

Method

In a bowl, combine all the ingredients for the stuffing and mix well. Spoon it into the stomach cavity of the chicken. In a pan, heat the oil and fry the stuffed chicken until it is golden brown all over. Set aside. In the same pan, add the cardamoms, fennel seeds, cinnamon sticks, cloves and onion paste. Cook for 30–60 seconds. Add the red chilli powder, black pepper, salt and ground coriander. Cook over a low heat for 5–10 minutes. Add the poppy seed, almond and coconut pastes and the hot water and bring to a boil. Add the chicken, cover and cook over a low heat for about 45 minutes until the chicken is cooked and tender, stirring occasionally. Remove the chicken from the pan and strain the sauce. Add the saffron, cream, nutmeg and vetivier to the sauce and mix well. Place the chicken on a serving platter. Pour the sauce over the chicken and garnish with flaked almonds and fresh coriander.

Chicken Stuffed with Nuts

Ingredients

One 2 lb chicken, skinned, ½ cup vegetable oil

8 cardamoms, 2 tsp fennel seeds

4 cinnamon sticks, 10 cloves

¾ cup onion paste (page 4)

2 tsp red chilli powder, 1 tsp ground black pepper

Salt, to taste, 2 tsp ground coriander

1 tbsp poppy seed paste (page 5)

1 tbsp almond paste (page 5)

¾ cup fresh coconut paste (page 5)

1 ¾ cup hot water

A pinch of saffron, 2 tbsp double cream

½ tsp ground nutmeg, 2 drops vetivier essence

1 oz flaked almonds, toasted, to garnish

2 tsp fresh coriander, chopped, to garnish

For the stuffing

1lb 12 oz chicken mince,

½ cup almonds, blanched

1 oz pistachio nuts, chopped

1 tbsp raisins, 3 tbsp brandy (optional)

4 tsp double cream

1 tsp ginger paste (page 7)

1 tsp green chilli paste (page 9)

½ tsp ground mace, Salt, to taste

Method

Heat the oil in a heavy-based saucepan over a medium heat. Add the bay leaves, cinnamon sticks, cardamoms, black cumin and cloves and cook until the spices begin to crackle. Add the onions, turmeric and yellow or red chilli powder and cook for 30 seconds. Add the ginger, garlic and cashew nut pastes and cook for a further 30 seconds. Add the chicken pieces and cook for 10–15 minutes over a medium heat, stirring occasionally. Add the yogurt with the hot water and salt. Cover and simmer for 10–15 minutes on a very low heat, stirring occasionally.

Stir in the cream and ground cardamom. Garnish with hard-boiled eggs, fresh coriander, ginger juliennes and red pepper strips and serve.

Chicken Shahjahani

Ingredients

5 tbsp vegetable oil	One 2lb 4 oz chicken, skinned and cut into 8 pieces
2 bay leaves	¾ cup plain yogurt
3 cinnamon sticks	1 ¾ cup hot water
8 cardamoms	Salt, to taste
½ tsp ground black cumin	3 tbsp double cream
8 cloves	½ tsp ground black cardamom
1 cup onions, chopped	
1 tsp ground turmeric	
2 tsp yellow or red chilli powder	**To garnish**
2 tbsp ginger paste (page 4)	3 eggs, hard boiled and quartered
2 tbsp garlic paste (page 4)	1 tbsp fresh coriander, chopped
½ cup cashew nut paste (page 5)	1 tsp ginger juliennes
	½ red pepper, cut into strips

Method

Cut the chicken into 15 pieces, skin and set aside. Whisk the yogurt in a large bowl, add the chicken and salt and stir to mix. Marinate the chicken in the yogurt mixture for at least 30 minutes. Heat the oil in a heavy-based pan. Add the whole spices (cardamoms, cloves, cinnamon sticks and bay leaves) and cook over a medium heat for a few minutes. Add the black cumin and onions and cook until golden brown. Add the garlic, ginger and green chillies and stir-fry for 2 minutes. Add the turmeric, coriander and red chilli powder and stir to mix.

Add 4 tbsp water and stir-fry for 30 seconds. Add the tomatoes and cook over a medium heat until the oil separates from the mixture. Add the marinated chicken along with the marinade ¾ cup water. Bring to a boil, cover and simmer for about 30 minutes, until the chicken is cooked and tender and the oil separates from the sauce once again. Adjust the seasoning. Sprinkle the ground fenugreek, mace, garam masala, ginger juliennes and fresh coriander over the chicken mixture. (If using fresh fenugreek, chop and cook it with the chicken.) Cover and cook for a further 5 minutes. Serve hot, garnished with fresh coriander.

Ingredients

2 lb 4 oz boneless chicken

8 z plain yogurt

Salt, to taste

¾ cup vegetable oil

10 cardamoms

2 black cardamoms

8 cloves

2 cinnamon sticks

2 bay leaves

½ tsp black cumin

2 tbsp onions, chopped

2 tbsp garlic, chopped

4 tbsp root ginger, peeled and chopped

1 tbsp green chillies, slit, seeded and chopped

1 tsp ground turmeric

1 ½ tsp ground coriander

1 ½ tsp red chilli powder

6 oz tomatoes, skinned and chopped

1 tbsp ground fenugreek, or 7 oz fresh fenugreek

1 tsp ground mace

Murgh Kastoori

2 tsp garam masala (page 5)

2 tsp ginger juliennes

1 tbsp fresh coriander, chopped, plus extra for garnishing

Variation

Use lamb or pork in place of chicken.

Method

Clean and skin the chicken. Cut it into 8 pieces. Heat the oil in a heavy-based pan over a medium heat. Add the bay leaves, cinnamon sticks, cardamoms and cloves and cook until they begin to crackle. Add the chopped onions, turmeric and red chilli powder and cook for a further 30 seconds. Add the ginger, garlic and cashew nut pastes and cook for a further 30 seconds. Add the chicken pieces, stir and cook for 10–15 minutes over a medium heat. Add the salt, yogurt and 2 tbsp hot water. Cover and simmer for 10 minutes over a low heat.

Add the cream, garam masala and fenugreek. Continue to cook for 2–3 minutes, stirring. To serve, transfer the chicken to a serving platter and garnish with the fresh coriander.

Creamy Chicken Curry

Ingredients

2lb 4 oz chicken

5 tbsp vegetable oil

2 bay leaves

3 cinnamon sticks

8 cardamoms

8 cloves

1 cup onions, chopped

1 tsp ground turmeric

1 ½ tsp red chilli powder

2 tbsp ginger paste (page 4)

2 tbsp garlic paste (page 4)

½ cup cashew nut paste (page 4)1 tbsp salt

¾ cup plain yogurt

5 tbsp double cream

1 tbsp garam masala (page 5)

½ tsp ground fenugreek

1 tbsp chopped fresh coriander, to garnish

Serving suggestion

Serve with stir-fried okra and basmati rice.

Method

Clean and cut the chicken into 8 pieces. Crush the peppercorns with a pestle and mortar to form a powder. Whisk the yogurt and add the ground peppercorns, half the ginger and garlic pastes, lemon juice and salt. Mix well. Add the chicken pieces, stir to mix and set aside to marinate for at least 30 minutes.

Meanwhile, heat the oil in a wok (kadhai). Add the onions and cook over a medium heat until lightly browned. Add the remaining ginger and garlic pastes and cook until the onions are golden brown, stirring occasionally. Add the tomatoes and stir-fry until the fat appears on the sides of the pan. Add the chicken along with the marinade and stir-fry for 4–5 minutes. Add 1 cup water and bring to a boil. Cover and simmer, stirring occasionally, until the chicken is cooked and tender. Adjust the seasoning. Sprinkle the garam masala over the top and stir to mix. Garnish with curry leaves or fresh coriander and serve.

Ingredients

One 2 lb 12 oz chicken

4 tsp black peppercorns

½ cup plain yogurt

3 tbsp ginger paste (page 4)

3 tbsp garlic paste (page 4)

2 tbsp lemon juice

Salt, to taste

4 tbsp peanut oil

¾ cup onions, chopped

¾ cup tomatoes, skinned and chopped

1 tsp garam masala (page 5)

Curry leaves or chopped fresh coriander, to garnish

Pepper Chicken

Variation

Use lime juice in place of the lemon juice and add some finely
grated zest for a sharper flavor.

Method

Debone, skin and cut the meat into 1 ½-in cubes. Mix the red chilli powder, turmeric and salt with half the ginger and garlic pastes.

Rub this marinade on to the chicken pieces. Cover and set aside for 30 minutes.

Heat the oil in a wok (kadhai), add the marinated chicken and cook over medium heat until lightly browned all over. Remove the chicken and reserve the oil.

Soak the tamarind in 5 tsp water. After 10 minutes, mash well, squeeze out the pulp and discard. Set the juice extract aside. Reheat the reserved oil, add the curry leaves and cook over a low heat for 30 seconds. Add the onions and cook until lightly browned. Add the remaining ginger and garlic pastes. Stir for 1 minute, then add the tomatoes and stir again. Cook until the fat appears on the sides of the pan. Add the cardamom, ground coriander, cloves and cinnamon and stir for 1 minute. Add the tamarind and cook for 5 minutes, stirring occasionally. Add the chicken pieces and simmer for 8–10 minutes. Add 1 cup water and bring to a boil. Reduce to a medium heat and cook, stirring constantly, until the moisture has evaporated and the sauce coats the chicken pieces. Sprinkle with pepper and lemon juice. Garnish with fresh coriander.

Fried Chicken Curry

Ingredients

One 2lb 12 oz chicken

½ tsp red chilli powder

1 tsp ground turmeric

Salt, to taste

3 tbsp ginger paste (page 4)

2 tbsp garlic paste (page 4)

5 tbsp groundnut oil, 2 tbsp tamarind

12 curry leaves, ½ cup onions, chopped

4 ½ oz tomatoes, skinned and chopped

½ tsp ground cardamom

½ tsp ground coriander

¼ tsp ground cloves, ¼ tsp ground cinnamon

½ tsp black peppercorns, crushed

1 tbsp lemon juice

4 tsp chopped fresh coriander leaves, to garnish

chicken

Method

Melt half the butter in a heavy-based saucepan. Add the cinnamon, cardamoms and bay leaf and cook for 30 seconds. Stir in the ginger and garlic pastes and cook until the juices evaporate. Add the tomatoes and salt and cook until the tomatoes are pulped. Add 1 ¾ cup water, bring to a boil and simmer for 20 minutes. Strain the juices through a sieve into another pan. Melt the remaining butter in a wok (kadhai). Add the ginger juliennes and green chillies and cook for 1 minute. Add the paprika – the color of the mixture will turn a bright red. Add the strained juices and bring to a boil. Add the tandoori chicken pieces and simmer for 10 minutes until the chicken is thoroughly heated through. Stir in the cream and honey and serve garnished with fresh coriander.

Ingredients

½ cup butter

2 cinnamon sticks

10 cardamoms

1 bay leaf

4 tbsp ginger paste (page 4)

4 tbsp garlic paste (page 4)

2 lb tomatoes, skinned and chopped

Salt, to taste

2 tsp ginger juliennes

5 green chillies, slit and seeded

1 tsp paprika

1 lb 4 oz tandoori chicken

¾ cup double cream

1 tbsp honey

1 tbsp chopped fresh coriander, to garnish

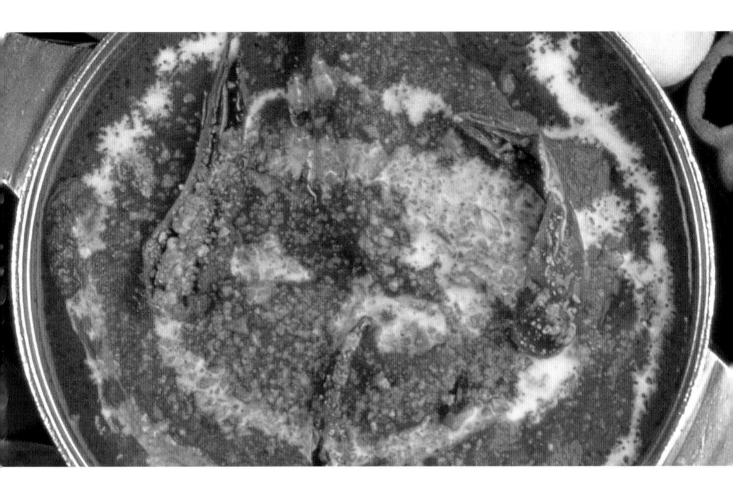

Butter Chicken

Serving suggestion

Serve with any Indian breads.

Method

Heat 1 tbspbof the clarified butter or ghee in a frying pan. Add the almonds and brown all over. Remove the pan from the heat and set aside.

Clean and flatten the chicken breasts until about ½ in thick. Rub the ginger paste over the chicken steaks. Whisk the yogurt in a large bowl, add the garlic paste and salt, then rub this mixture into the chicken. Cover and set aside for 1 hour. Preheat a wok (kadhai). Place half the remaining clarified butter or ghee in it. Add the chicken breasts and cook, turning once, until semi-cooked. Remove from the wok and set aside. Add the remaining clarified butter or ghee to the pan and cook the cardamoms and cloves until they crackle. Add the onions and cook until brown. Add the tomatoes, red chilli powder, flour, black pepper and chicken stock. Cook until the sauce becomes rich and thick, stirring occasionally. Place the chicken in the sauce and cook, turning it over gently, for a further 10 minutes. Stir in the mace and saffron. Serve garnished with the fried almonds and fresh coriander.

Ingredients

½ cup clarified butter or ghee

1 oz almonds, blanched and sliced

8 boneless, skinless chicken breasts

4 tbsp ginger paste (page 4)

1 cup plain yogurt

4 tbsp garlic paste (page 4)

Salt, to taste

10 cardamoms

10 cloves

½ cup onions, chopped

9 oz tomatoes, skinned and chopped

1 tsp red chilli powder

2 tsp plain flour

½ tsp ground black pepper

4 cups chicken stock

½ tsp ground mace

A pinch of saffron, dissolved in 1 tbsp milk

4 tsp chopped fresh coriander, to garnish

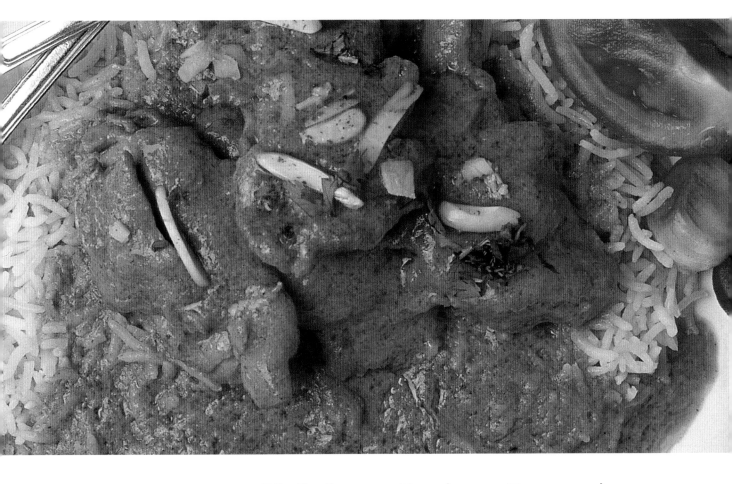

Chicken Badam Pasanda

Serving suggestion

Serve with rice.

Method

Heat the oil in a wok (kadhai) and cook the garlic paste until brown. Add the ground chillies and coriander seeds and stir-fry for a few seconds.

Add the tomatoes and bring to a boil. Add half the coriander leaves and all the ginger, green chillies and salt. Simmer for 5 minutes. Add the chicken and simmer, stirring occasionally, until the sauce thickens and the chicken is cooked and tender. Once the fat rises to the surface, stir in the garam masala and cook for 2 minutes. Garnish with the remaining fresh coriander and ginger juliennes.

Ingredients

5 tbsp vegetable oil

4 tsp garlic paste

8 whole dried red chillies, roughly ground

1 tsp coriander seeds, roughly ground

2 lb 4 oz tomatoes, skinned and chopped

2 tbsp fresh coriander leaves

3 tbsp root ginger, peeled and chopped

4 green chillies, slit

Salt, to taste

2 lb 4 oz chickens, each cut into 8 pieces

2 tsp garam masala (page 5)

Ginger juliennes, to garnish

Kadhai Chicken

Serving suggestion

Serve with naan or chapattis.

Preparation

Heat the oil up in a wok over a mild heat and stir-fry the onions, lemongrass and lime leaves for 3 minutes or until the onions are golden.

Add the curry paste and, optionally, the shrimp paste, and stir-fry for another 3 minutes. Stir in the coconut milk, fish sauce and sugar and bring to a boil. Lower the temperature and allow to simmer for 10 minutes, while stirring continuously.

Add the chicken, bamboo sprouts, sweet corn and basil and cook for a further 15 minutes, while stirring continuously, until the chicken is tender.

Ingredients

1 tbs peanut oil

1 onion, chopped

1 stem fresh lemongrass, finely chopped

or 1 tsp dried lemongrass, soaked in water until soft

3 kafir lime leaves, finely chopped

2 tbs Thai green curry paste

1 tsp prawn paste (optional)

2 cups coconut milk

1 tbs Thai fish sauce (nam pla)

1 tbs sugar

2 lbs chicken thigh or chicken breast filet, cut into 1-inch cubes

8 oz bamboo sprouts (can), drained

8 oz sweet baby corn (can), drained

2 tbs fresh basil, chopped

Chicken with Coconut

chicken

Method

Heat the oil in a pan, add the whole spices (cinnamon and bay leaves) and cook over a medium heat until they begin to crackle. Add the ginger, garlic and onion pastes and red chilli powder and cook for 30–60 seconds. Add the tomatoes and cook for 1 minute. Add the spinach purée, stir in the maize flour diluted with 3 tbsp water and cook over a medium heat for 10–15 minutes, stirring occasionally. In a separate pan, heat the butter and cook the chicken until lightly browned all over. Transfer the chicken pieces into the spinach sauce. Add salt and white pepper, cover and simmer over a very low heat for 10–15 minutes or until the chicken is cooked and tender. Serve garnished with ginger juliennes and ground fenugreek.

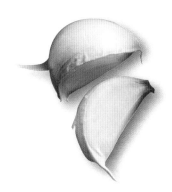

Saag Murgh

Ingredients

4 tbsp vegetable oil

4 cinnamon sticks

2 bay leaves

½ oz ginger paste (page 4)

1 ½ oz garlic paste (page 4)

1 cup onion paste (page 5)

2 tsp red chilli powder

6 oz tomatoes, skinned and chopped

12 oz cooked spinach, puréed

½ tsp maize flour

3 ½ oz butter

One 2 lb 4 oz chicken, skinned and cut into small pieces

Salt, to taste

½ tsp white pepper

2 tsp ginger juliennes, to garnish

½ tsp ground fenugreek, to garnish

Variation

Use puréed peas in place of the spinach.

chicken

Method

Place the lamb into a pan of water and bring to a boil. Drain and wash the pieces of meat. Place the blanched lamb pieces, chopped onions, ginger and garlic pastes, yogurt, butter, chillies, salt and half the ground cardamom in a pan. Bring to a boil and simmer for 1–1½ hours, stirring occasionally, until the lamb is cooked and tender. Add the almond paste and cook gently until the gravy thickens. Add the remaining ground cardamom, sweet ittar and cream, stir to mix and serve. Sprinkle with saffron crushed in a little water, garnish with ginger juliennes and serve.

Ingredients

2 lb lean lamb, diced

½ cup onions, chopped

2 tsp ginger paste (page 4)

2 tsp garlic paste (page 4)

2 oz plain yogurt

2 oz unsalted butter

2 green chillies, chopped

Salt, to taste

1 tsp ground cardamom

2 tbsp almond paste

A few drops of sweet ittar

2 tbsp double cream

A pinch of saffron

Ginger juliennes, to garnish

Cardamom-Flavored Lamb

Serving suggestion

Serve with Indian bread such as naan or paratha.

Method

Whisk together the yogurt and salt. Add the lamb and stir to mix. Cover and set aside to marinate for 1 hour. Heat the oil in a saucepan, add the bay leaves and cardamoms and heat until crackling. Add the onions and cook until lightly browned. Add the ginger and garlic pastes and stir-fry for 4–5 minutes. Stir in the coriander, turmeric and red chilli powder. Add the lamb with the marinade, bring to a boil, then reduce the heat. Simmer, adding 1 tbsp water occasionally, for about 30 minutes. Add the tomatoes, chopped garlic and shredded ginger and stir to mix. Add the cumin and whole red chillies.

Cook over a low heat for 30–45 minutes until the lamb pieces are coated with the sauce and are cooked and tender.

Garnish with coriander and tomato slices and serve.

Rara Meat

Ingredients

¾ cup plain yogurt

Salt, to taste

2 lb 4 oz lean lamb, cut into cubes

¾ cup vegetable oil

2 bay leaves

3 black cardamoms

8 cardamoms

1 cup onions, chopped

3 tbsp ginger paste (page 4)

3 tbsp garlic paste (page 4)

5 tsp ground coriander

½ tsp ground turmeric

1 tsp red chilli powder

6 oz tomatoes, skinned and chopped

4 tsp garlic, chopped

4 tsp root ginger, peeled and shredded

2 tsp ground cumin

4 whole red chillies

Chopped fresh coriander and tomato slices, to garnish

Serving suggestion

Serve with any Indian bread.

Method

Mix together half the ginger and garlic pastes. Add the lamb, stir to coat all over, then cover and set aside to marinate for 2 hours. In a non-stick pan, heat the oil and cook the unions until lightly browned. Add the remaining ginger and garlic pastes, cumin seeds, salt, poppy seeds, cashew nuts, green chillies and the whole spices (cinnamon, cloves, black pepper-corns and bay leaf). Cook for 5 minutes over a moderate heat. Add the lamb and cook for 8–10 minutes. Every few minutes, sprinkle with 1 tbsp water to keep the contents of the pan moist. Add 2 cups water and the potatoes. Cover, bring to a boil and simmer for 1–1 ½ hours, until the lamb is cooked and tender, stirring occasionally. Add the coconut milk, simmer for 1 minute, then remove from the heat. Garnish with the coriander and pepper pieces and serve.

Ingredients

2 tsp ginger paste (page 4)

2 tsp garlic paste (page 4)

1 lb 2 oz stewing lamb, diced

5 tbsp vegetable oil

¾ cup onions, chopped

½ tsp cumin seeds

Salt, to taste

½ tsp poppy seeds

3 oz cashew nuts

4 green chillies

1 cinnamon stick

4 cloves

½ tsp black peppercorns

1 bay leaf

6 oz potatoes, diced

1 cup + 2 tbsp coconut milk

Fresh coriander leaves, red and green pepper pieces, to garnish

Kid nu Gosht

Serving suggestion

Serve hot with steamed rice.

lamb

Method

Clean the lamb chops and remove and discard excess fat. Pat dry with a kitchen paper towel, sprinkle with salt and set aside for 10 minutes. Heat the oil in a pan, add the sugar, cloves, bay leaves, cardamoms and cinnamon sticks and cook for 2–3 minutes. Add the lamb chops and cook over a medium heat until the chops are lightly browned all over. Add the chopped onions and cook until browned.

Add the red chilli powder, black cumin seeds, chopped tomatoes and ginger paste and fry until the oil separates from the sauce. Add the stock or water, bring to a boil and cook for about 30 minutes until the chops are tender. Add the ground fennel seeds and cover and simmer for 10 minutes over a low heat.

Serve immediately, garnished with a pinch of ground fennel seeds.

Ingredients

2 lb 4 oz lamb chops

Salt, to taste

4 tbsp vegetable oil

1 tsp sugar

10 cloves

3 bay leaves

8 cardamoms

2 cinnamon sticks

¾ cup onions, chopped

2 tsp red chilli powder

1/2 tsp black cumin seeds

14 oz tomatoes, skinned, seeded and chopped

2 tsp ginger paste (page 4)

1 cup lamb stock or water

1 tsp ground fennel seeds

Lamb Rogan Josh

Method

Heat the oil in a saucepan. Add the cinnamon, cardamoms, cloves and bay leaf and cook over a medium heat for 30 seconds. Add the ginger, garlic and green chilli pastes and cook for 2 minutes. Add the yogurt and lamb and cook over a low heat for 45 minutes, stirring occasionally, until the lamb is cooked and tender. Add the cashew nut paste, salt, pepper and saffron. Stir briefly, then remove from the heat. Serve garnished with chopped fresh coriander and cashew nuts.

Lamb Mughlai

Ingredients

1 cup vegetable oil

4 cinnamon sticks

6 cardamoms

8 cloves

1 bay leaf

4 tbsp ginger paste (page 4)

4 tbsp garlic paste (page 4)

4 tbsp green chilli paste (page 5)

½ cup plain yogurt

2 lb 4 oz lamb chops or cutlets

10 ½ oz cashew nut paste (page 5)

Salt, to taste

½ tsp ground black pepper

A pinch of saffron

Chopped fresh coriander and coarsely chopped cashew nuts, to garnish

Serving suggestion

Serve with parathas or naan.

Method

Soak the almonds in boiling water, then set aside. Soak the cashew nuts and poppy seeds in water for 1 hour. Blend all 3 with a little water to a fine paste in a blender or food processor and set aside. Heat the oil in a wok (kadhai) and cook the onions and garlic over a low heat without letting them brown. Add the mince and cook over a gentle heat until browned all over.

Whisk and add the yogurt, ground cardamom, white pepper and whole green chillies and stir to mix. Bring to a boil and simmer gently for about 25 minutes until the mince is cooked and the sauce is reduced by half, stirring occasionally. Remove and discard the green chillies. Add the nut paste and stir well. Simmer for a further 2–3 minutes. Serve immediately, garnished with the pepper pieces.

Ingredients

1 tbsp blanched almonds

1 tbsp unsalted cashew nuts

1 tbsp poppy seeds

4 tbsp vegetable oil

½ cup onions, chopped

1 tbsp garlic, chopped

1 lb 10 oz minced lamb

1 cup plain yogurt

½ tsp ground cardamom

1 tsp ground white pepper

4 whole green chillies

Diamond-shaped pieces of red and green pepper, to garnish

White Mince

Serving suggestion

Serve hot with paratha.

Method

Wash and dry the lamb and cut into small cubes. Rub the ginger and garlic pastes over the lamb and set aside for 1 hour. Heat the clarified butter or ghee and unsalted butter in a pan. Add the bay leaves, cinnamon sticks

and cardamoms and cook until they crackle. Add the onions and cook until soft.

Add the cubed lamb and cook over a high heat until the lamb changes color.

Add the yogurt and almond paste and cook over a low heat for a further 25 minutes, or until the lamb cubes are tender. Add the cream, green chillies to taste, ground white pepper, salt and ground cardamom. Heat gently for 2–3 minutes, stirring. Sprinkle with turmeric before serving.

Gosht Shahi Korma

Ingredients

2 lb 4 oz lean boneless lamb

2 tbsp ginger paste (page 4)

2 tbsp garlic paste (page 4)

¾ cup clarified butter or ghee

½ cup unsalted butter

2 bay leaves

5 cinnamon sticks

10 cardamoms

¾ cups onions, sliced

1 cup plain yogurt

4 tbsp almond paste

½ cup double cream

6–10 green chillies, seeded and sliced

½ tsp ground white pepper

Salt, to taste

½ tsp ground cardamom

½ tsp ground turmeric, to garnishc

Serving suggestion

Serve with pulao rice and Indian bread.

Method

Clean and cut the lamb into 1 ¼-in cubes. Place in a pan, add the salt and

6 cups boiling water and boil for 5 minutes. Drain and wash the lamb. Set aside. Mix

the yogurt and white pepper together, then set aside. Place the almonds and

coconut in a blender or food processor, add 4 tbsp water

and blend for 4–5 minutes to form a fine paste. Heat the oil in a pan, add the

blanched lamb, the spiced yogurt, ginger juliennes, salt 3 ½ cups water.

Cover, bring to a boil and simmer for 30–45 minutes, stirring occasionally, until the

lamb is cooked and tender and the liquid has almost evaporated.

Add the almond and coconut paste and cook for 2 minutes. Add the ground cardamom and stir to mix. Add the cream, lemon juice, rose water and chopped green

chillies and stir to mix. Cover the pan tightly and place in a preheated oven at 350 °F

for 15 minutes. To serve, transfer the cooked lamb to a shallow dish.

Ingredients

3 lb 5 oz boneless lamb

Salt, to taste

1 cup plain yogurt

1 tsp ground white pepper

4 tbsp almonds, blanched

4 tbsp fresh coconut pieces

¾ cup vegetable oil

4 tsp ginger juliennes

½ tsp ground white cardamom

4 tbsp double cream

2 tsp lemon juice

1 tsp rose water

6 green chillies, chopped

Safed Maas

lamb

Variation

Use hazelnuts or cashew nuts in place of almonds.

Method

Fry the onions with a little clarified butter or ghee. Cool slightly, then grind to a paste in a blender or food processor and set aside. In the same pan, heat the remaining clarified butter or ghee and add the lamb, cardamoms, cloves, cinnamon, bay leaves, ginger and garlic pastes and salt. Cover and cook over a low heat for 30 minutes, stirring occasionally. Uncover and stir-fry for a few minutes until the liquid evaporates. Add the yogurt and continue to stir-fry until the liquid evaporates again. n

Add the red chilli powder, dissolved in 2 tbsp water, and stir for 1 minute.

Add the fried onion paste dissolved in 3 tbsp water and continue to fry.

Add 1 tbsp water when the liquid evaporates, to ensure that the sauce and the lamb do not burn. Add the pepper and cumin, 5 cups water and bring to a boil. Cover tightly, lower the heat and simmer for about 1 ½ hours, stirring occasionally, until the lamb is cooked and tender. Remove the lamb from the sauce. Strain the sauce, return to the pan and boil the sauce rapidly until it reaches pouring consistency. Add the mace, ground cardamom and the saffron with the vetivier mixed in the milk. Cook for 5 minutes.

To serve, pour the sauce over the lamb and garnish with ginger juliennes and fresh coriander leaves.

Kohe Awadh

Ingredients

¾ cup onions, chopped

4 tbsp clarified butter or ghee

2 lb 4 oz lamb meat from the shanks,on the bone, cut into 10 pieces, 8 cardamoms

8 cloves, 2 cinnamon sticks

2 bay leaves, 3 tbsp ginger paste (page 4)

3 tbsp garlic paste (page 4)

14 oz plain yogurt

1 tsp red chilli powder

1 tsp ground black pepper

¼ tsp ground cumin, 1 tsp ground mace

¼ tsp) ground cardamom

1 tsp saffron

2 drops vetivier

1 tbsp milk

2 tsp ginger juliennes, to garnish

Fresh coriander leaves, to garnish

lamb

Method

Clean and cut the lamb into small pieces with the bone. Heat ½ cup of the oil in a wok (kadhai), add the sliced onions and cook over a medium heat until golden brown. Add the lamb, chopped onions, cardamoms, cloves, cinnamon, black peppercorns and bay leaves and cook until the liquid evaporates, stirring occasionally. Add the ground coriander, red chillies, turmeric, ginger and garlic pastes and salt and cook until the oil separates from the mixture.

Add the yogurt, bring to a boil, reduce the heat to medium and cook for 10 minutes.Add 4 cups water and bring to a boil again. Cover and simmer for about 30 minutes, stirring occasionally, until the lamb is tender. Remove the meat from the sauce, cover and set aside. Heat the remaining oil in a pan, add the flour and gram flour and cook over a low heat, stirring constantly, until lightly browned. Add the sauce and stir until thickened. Pour the thickened sauce through a sieve, return to the pan and bring to the boil. Add the lamb, garam masala, ground fennel, lemon juice, vetivier, saffron and mace and stir to mix. Garnish with fresh coriander and serve.

Ingredients

2 lb 4 oz lamb on the bone (any cut)

¾ cup mustard oil

1 cup onions, sliced

1 cup onions, chopped

10 cardamoms

10 cloves

4 cinnamon sticks

20 black peppercorns

2 bay leaves

4 tsp ground coriander

8 whole red chillies

2 tsp ground turmeric

1 tsp ginger paste (page 4)

1 tsp garlic paste (page 4)

Salt, to taste

1 cup plain yogurt

1 tsp plain flour

1 tsp gram flour

2 tsp garam masala (page 5)

1 tsp ground fennel

1 tsp lemon juice

1 tbsp vetivier

A pinch of saffron

½ tsp ground mace

1 tbsp chopped fresh coriander, to garnish

Nahari Gosht

Serving suggestion

Serve with Indian bread such as naan or paratha.

lamb

49

Method

Heat half the oil in a wok (kadhai) and cook half the onions until golden brown. Remove from the pan and set aside. Peel and chop the ginger and garlic. Mix with the browned and raw onions and poppy seeds, then blend in a food processor or blender to a fine paste with 2 tbsp water. Heat the remaining oil in the wok (kadhai) and heat the black cardamoms, cinnamon, bay leaf and cloves until they crackle. Add the blended paste and cook for 3–4 minutes. Add the yogurt and cook for 4–5 minutes. Add the lamb and cook for a further 3–4 minutes until the fat rises to the surface, stirring occasionally. Transfer to a casserole dish. Add ½ cup water and stir to mix. Sprinkle the red chilli powder, garam masala, ground cardamom and black pepper over the top. Cover and cook in a preheated oven at 400°F for 15 minutes. Garnish with fresh coriander and serve.

Lamb with Whole Spices

Ingredients

8 tbsp vegetable oil

9 oz onions, sliced

1 oz root ginger

3 tbsp garlic cloves

1 tbsp poppy seeds

2 black cardamoms

1 cinnamon stick

1 bay leaf

6 cloves

1 cup plain yogurt

1 lb 10 oz lamb escalopes 2 x 4 in

1 tsp red chilli powder

1 tsp garam masala (page 5)

½ tsp ground cardamom

½ tsp ground black pepper

1 tsp chopped fresh coriander, to garnish

Serving suggestion

Serve hot with sliced onion rings, quartered tomatoes, shredded crisp lettuce and naan.

Method

For the dumplings, knead the grated paneer until it is of a smooth and creamy texture. Add the mashed potatoes, coriander, mixed nuts, turmeric, asafoetida, ginger, green chillies, dry mango powder, lemon juice, salt and cornflour and knead until the ingredients are thoroughly mixed. Lightly oil your hands and divide the mixture into 12 portions. Roll each portion into a ball. Place all the balls on a tray lined with plastic wrap, cover and set aside. Heat oil in a wok (kadhai) to 350°F. Slide in a few balls at a time and fry until golden brown all over. Remove from the oil, drain excess oil on kitchen paper towels and set aside. For the curry, place the nuts, ginger, green chillies, ground coriander, cumin and turmeric in a blender or food processor and blend with enough water to make a smooth paste. Set aside. Heat the clarified butter or ghee in a heavy-based pan over a moderate heat. Stir-fry the cumin seeds, cinnamon stick and cloves for 10–15 seconds. Stir in half the tomatoes and the prepared paste and cook until the liquid from the tomatoes evaporates and the oil separates. Add the remaining tomatoes, 1 cup water and salt. Cover the pan and simmer for 10–15 minutes, or until the curry has thickened slightly.

Carefully stir in the dumplings and bring the curry to a boil. Spoon the dumplings into a serving dish, pour the curry over the top and garnish with cream. Serve.

Ingredients

For the dumplings

1 lb 2 oz paneer (page 4), grated	1–2 green chillies, seeded and finely chopped
3–4 potatoes, boiled and mashed	
3 tbsp fresh coriander, chopped	½ tsp dry mango powder
3 tbsp mixed nuts, finely chopped	1 tsp lemon juice
½ tsp ground turmeric	1 ½ tsp salt
A pinch of ground asafoetida	2 tbsp cornflour
1 tbsp root ginger, peeled and finely shredded	Vegetable oil, for frying

Potato and Paneer Dumplings in Curry

For the curry

1 ½ oz cashew nuts or almonds, finely chopped

1 tbsp root ginger, peeled and finely chopped

2 green chillies, chopped

1 ½ tsp ground coriander

1 tsp ground cumin

½ tsp ground turmeric

5 tbsp clarified butter or ghee

1 tsp cumin seeds

1 cinnamon stick

4 cloves

1 lb 5 oz tomatoes, skinned and finely chopped

Salt, to taste

Double cream, to garnish

Method

Whisk the yogurt, salt, red chilli powder, turmeric and half the gram flour together in a bowl. Set aside. Sift the remaining gram flour and bicarbonate of soda together, add the carom seeds and add enough water to make a thick batter. Beat well. Add the green chillies. Heat enough oil in a wok (kadhai) to deep-fry. Drop large spoonfuls of the batter in the oil to make 1 ½-in puffy dumplings. Fry until golden brown on both sides. Remove and set aside. Heat 3 tbsp peanut oil in a pan, add the yogurt mixture and 3 cups water. Bring to a boil, reduce to a low heat and simmer for 8–10 minutes, stirring constantly, to prevent the yogurt curdling. Add the potatoes and onions and cook until the potatoes are cooked and tender. Add the dumplings and simmer for 3 minutes.

Heat the remaining 1 tbsp oil in a small frying pan. Add the cumin, mustard and fenugreek seeds and cook until the cumin crackles. Add the whole red chillies and stir. Pour over the simmering hot curry. Serve garnished with the red and green chillies.

Kadhi

Ingredients

1 ½ cups plain yogurt

Salt, to taste

1 tsp red chilli powder

1 tsp ground turmeric

4 ½ oz gram flour

A pinch of bicarbonate of soda

½ tsp carom seeds

5 green chillies, chopped

Vegetable oil, for deep-frying

4 tbsp peanut oil

5 ½ oz potatoes, cut into rounds about 5 mm (¼ in) thick

¾ cup onions, cut into 1/4-in thick slices

½ tsp cumin seeds

¼ tsp mustard seeds

¼ tsp fenugreek seeds

4 whole red chillies

Whole red and green chillies, to garnish

vegetarian

Method

Place the plantains in a pan, cover with boiling water and boil for 30 minutes. Cool, peel and mash. Mix in the finely chopped onion and ginger, coriander, green chillies, white pepper and salt. Divide the mixture into 15 portions and roll into balls between your palms. Deep-dry in a wok (kadhai) over a low heat until golden brown all over. Set aside and keep warm. Remove excess oil from the wok (kadhai) reserving 4 tbsp. Heat the oil and the cardamoms, cloves and cinnamon and cook until they begin to crackle. Add the roughly chopped onions and cook until transparent. Add the ginger and garlic pastes and cook until the onions turn brown. Purée the tomatoes in a blender or food processor. Add the tomato purée, red chilli powder and salt to the wok (kadhai) and stir-fry until the oil rises to the surface. Add 1 ¾ cup water. Bring to a boil, remove from the heat and strain through a sieve into another pan. Place the pan on the heat and bring the sauce to a boil. Add the cream. Remove from the heat and add the honey. Arrange the koftas in an ovenproof casserole dish. Pour the sauce over, sprinkle with ground mace and tightly cover the dish. Bake in a preheated oven at 400°F for 10 minutes. Serve immediately garnished with ginger juliennes and fresh coriander.

Ingredients

l lb plantains

4 tbsp onions, finely chopped

1 tbsp root ginger, peeled and finely chopped

4 tsp fresh coriander, chopped

6 green chillies, finely chopped

½ tsp ground white pepper

Salt, to taste

Vegetable oil, for deep-frying

6 cardamoms

4 cloves

1 cinnamon stick

4 tbsp onions, roughly chopped

1 tbsp ginger paste (page 4)

1 tbsp garlic paste (page 4)

6 oz tomatoes, skinned and chopped

1 tsp red chilli powder

4 tbsp double cream

1 tsp honey

A pinch of ground mace

Ginger juliennes and chopped fresh coriander, to garnish

Plantain Kofta

Serving suggestion

Serve with boiled rice or paratha.

Method

Cut the paneer into fingers and set aside. Cut the green pepper in half, remove the seeds and make juliennes or cut into small, even squares. Set aside.

Pound the red chillies and coriander seeds with a pestle and mortar to form a powder. Heat the oil in a wok (kadhai) and cook the onions and green pepper over a medium heat for 2 minutes. Add the pounded spices and ⅔ of the ginger juliennes and cook for 1 minute, stirring. Add the tomato purée and salt, bring to a boil and simmer until the oil separates from the sauce. Add the paneer and cook gently for 2–3 minutes, stirring. Sprinkle with fenugreek, garam masala, ground coriander and black pepper and stir to mix. To serve, garnish with fresh coriander and the remaining ginger juliennes.

Kadhai Paneer

Ingredients

1 lb 5 oz paneer (page 4)

1 ½ oz green pepper

14 whole dried red chillies

2 tsp coriander seeds

3 tbsp vegetable oil

3 tbsp onions, chopped

1 tbsp ginger juliennes

¾ cup tomato purée

Salt, to taste

1 tsp ground fenugreek

2 tsp garam masala (page 5)

2 tsp ground coriander

2 tsp ground black pepper

1 tbsp chopped fresh coriander, to garnish

Serving suggestion

Serve with paratha and a mixed salad or raita (plain yogurt mixed with a little chopped cucumber, onion, chopped fresh coriander and ground cumin).

Method

Bring the coriander roots, lemongrass, lime leaves, sugar, water and fish sauce to a boil in a steel pan. Lower the temperature and leave to simmer for 10 minutes. Remove the larger pieces by running the broth through a sieve.

Heat the oil in a wok or large steel pan over a mild heat and stir-fry the ginger, curry paste and peppers (optional) for 2-3 minutes or until the flavor starts coming through. Add the beans and stir so as to cover them with the herb mixture. Add the broth and leave to simmer for 10 minutes or until the vegetables are soft.

Add the tomatoes and tamarind and leave to simmer for a further 3 minutes until everything has heated up. Add the mint as the final ingredient.

Ingredients

6 coriander plants, with the roots separated and washed

2 stems of fresh, chopped lemongrass or 1 tsp dried lemongrass,

soaked in hot water until soft

6 kafir lime leaves, chopped

2 tsp Java sugar or brown sugar

3 cups water

3 tbs Thai fish sauce (nam pla)

2 tsp peanut oil

2 inches chopped ginger

3 small fresh green peppers, chopped (optional)

2 tsp Thai green curry paste

½ lbs black-eyed peas or green beans

1 lbs tomatoes (can), drained and crushed

2 tbs tamarind concentrate

2 oz fresh mint leaves

Bean Curry with Mint

Method

Heat the oil in a pan, add the cloves, bay leaves, cinnamon sticks and cardamoms and cook over a medium heat until they begin to crackle. Add the onion paste and stir-fry for 2–3 minutes. Stir in the ginger and garlic pastes, red chilli powder, turmeric, ground coriander, cashew nut paste, salt and food coloring. Add the yogurt, ½ cup warm water and sugar. Bring to a boil, then simmer until the oil separates. Remove the pan from the heat. Allow the curry to cool, then remove the whole spices and discard. Blend the curry to a smooth consistency in a blender or food processor. Return to the rinsed-out pan.

Reheat the curry, then stir in the cream, garam masala, ground cardamom, mace, vetivier and saffron mixture. Add the paneer fingers and cook for a further 5 minutes, stirring occasionally. Serve hot, garnished with fresh coriander.

Ingredients

5 tbsp vegetable oil	Salt, to taste
6 cloves	A few drops of red food coloring
2 bay leaves	¾ cup plain yogurt
3 cinnamon sticks	2 tsp sugar
6 cardamoms	½ cup double cream
1 cup onion paste (page 5)	2 tsp garam masala (page 5)
3 tbsp ginger paste (page 4)	½ tsp ground cardamom
3 tbsp garlic paste ((page 4)	½ tsp ground mace
2 tsp red chilli powder	A few drops of vetivier
1 tsp ground turmeric	A pinch of saffron, dissolved in 1 tbsp milk
1 tsp ground coriander	2 lb 4 oz paneer (page 5), cut into fingers
2 tsp cashew nut paste (page 5)	Chopped fresh coriander, to garnish

Shahi Paneer

Serving suggestion

Serve with any dry vegetable dish and parathas.

Method

Shell and devein the prawns, then wash and pat them dry. Set aside.

Blend the peppercorns, cardamoms, cinnamon, cloves, cumin and red chillies with the vinegar in a blender or food processor until smooth. Set aside.

Heat the oil in a wok (kadhai) and deep-fry the prawns until golden brown. Remove from the oil and set aside. Keep hot. Add the onions to the hot oil and cook until golden brown. Add the ginger and garlic pastes and stir-fry for 1 minute. Add the tomatoes and the blended paste and stir-fry for 2–3 minutes.

Add the fried prawns, curry leaves and sugar and cook for 5–10 minutes until the prawns are tender. Serve.

Prawn Balchao

Ingredients

2 lb 4 oz small prawns

½ tsp black peppercorns

12 cardamoms

4 cinnamon sticks

15 cloves

½ tsp cumin seeds

15 whole red chillies

¾ cup malt vinegar

¾ cup peanut oil

6 oz onions, chopped

1 tbsp ginger paste (page 4)

2 tbsp garlic paste (page 4)

4 ½ oz tomatoes, skinned and chopped

12 curry leaves

2 tbsp sugar

Variation

Use leeks in place of the onions.

Method

Sprinkle lemon juice over the fish and set aside for 30 minutes. Wash with fresh water, squeeze lightly and pat dry. Fry the fish lightly in oil and set aside. Keep hot. In a small pan, heat 1 tbsp oil. Add the dried spices and cook gently for 2 minutes. Set aside to cool, then blend to a smooth paste in a blender or food processor with the yogurt. Heat the remaining oil in a pan and cook the onions until brown. Add the garlic and ginger and stir-fry

for 4–5 minutes. Add the paste to the sauce and cook until the sauce thickens. Add the salt and curry leaves.

Gently add the fried fish to the curry and simmer for 5 minutes. Garnish with curry leaves.

Mahi Musallam

Ingredients

4 lb 8 oz whole river or sea fish, e.g. trout, salmon, cod or haddock

1 cup vegetable oil

1 cup onion paste (page 5)

4 tbsp ginger paste (page 4)

4 tbsp garlic paste (page 4)

1 tbsp ground coriander

2 tsp red chilli powder

2 tsp ground turmeric

¾ cup plain yogurt

1 tsp ground fenugreek

1 tbsp garam masala (page 5)

5 drops vetivier

1 tbsp lemon juice

2 tbsp melted butter, to garnish

For the marinade paste

4 tsp garlic paste (page 4)

4 tsp ginger paste (page 4)

1 tbsp lemon juice

1 tsp red chilli powder

Salt, to taste

Method

Remove the heads from the prawns and discard. Slit and devein the prawns, then wash and pat them dry. Mix the malt vinegar, salt, yellow or red chilli powder and ginger and garlic pastes together. Add the prawns, mix well and marinate for 30 minutes. Place each prawn on a separate 10-in square of greased aluminium foil. Boil, drain and crush the peas with a rolling pin. Mix in the grated cheese, onion, coriander, ginger, cumin, lemon juice, white pepper, tomato ketchup and pomegranate seeds. Top each prawn with some of this mixture. Grate a little extra cheese on each and wrap up in the foil. Place the parcels on a baking tray and bake in a preheated oven at 350°F for 10–12 minutes.

Serve hot garnished with ginger juliennes and green chillies.

Ingredients

1 lb 12 oz jumbo prawns

2 tbsp malt vinegar

Salt, to taste

½ tsp yellow or red chilli powder

2 tsp ginger paste (page 4)

2 tsp garlic paste (page 4)

4 ½ oz fresh peas

1 oz Cheddar cheese, grated, plus extra

2 oz pickled onions, chopped

2 tsp fresh coriander, chopped

1 tsp root ginger, peeled and finely chopped

1/2 tsp cumin seeds

2 tbsp lemon juice

1/2 tsp white pepper

3 tbsp tomato ketchup

9 oz fresh pomegranate seeds

Ginger juliennes and split green chillies, to garnish

Baked Prawns with Pomegranate (Jhinga Dum Anari)

fish & seafood

Serving suggestion

Serve with any Indian bread, such as naan.

Method

Mix together the ginger and garlic pastes, salt, lemon juice and half the red chilli powder in a bowl. Add the fish and stir to mix. Cover and set aside to marinate for 30 minutes. Meanwhile, blend the coconut, sunflower seeds and cashew nuts in a blender or food processor until smooth. Heat the oil in a pan. Add the fish and cook gently for 10 minutes, turning occasionally. Remove, set aside and keep hot. In the remaining hot oil, cook the peeled garlic until golden brown. Add the tomatoes and stir-fry until they are soft and pulpy.

Stir in the remaining red chilli powder and cook for 5 minutes. Strain the sauce through a sieve and return to the pan. Add the coconut, sunflower seed and cashew nut paste and stir for 2–3 minutes. Add the garam masala and the fried fish. Reserve 2 tbsp cream for garnishing and add the rest to the sauce.

Simmer for 2–3 minutes, stirring. Garnish with fresh coriander and the remaining cream. Serve hot.

Ingredients

1 tbsp ginger paste (page 4)

2 tsp garlic paste (page 4)

Salt, to taste

2 tbsp lemon juice

2 tsp red chilli powder

1 lb 5 oz sole fillets

2 tsp fresh coconut, grated

2 tsp sunflower seeds

2 tsp unsalted cashew nuts

½ cup vegetable oil

1 oz garlic, peeled and chopped

10 ½ oz tomatoes, skinned and chopped

1 tsp garam masala (page 5)

5 tbsp double cream

2 tsp chopped fresh coriander, to garnish

Fish in Tomato Sauce

Serving suggestion

Serve with sliced fresh tomatoes, cucumber slices and

lemon wedges accompanied by boiled or steamed rice.

Method

Sprinkle the lemon juice over the fish and set aside for 30 minutes. Wash with fresh water, squeeze lightly and pat dry. Fry the fish lightly in oil and set aside. Keep hot. In a small pan, heat 1 tbsp peanut oil. Add the mustard seeds, fenugreek seeds, cardamoms, cinnamon, cloves and whole red chillies and cook gently for 2 minutes. Set aside to cool, then blend to a smooth paste in a blender or food processor with the grated coconut. Mash the soaked tamarind with your fingers, then squeeze out and discard the pulp. Reserve the juices and set aside. Heat the remaining groundnut oil in a pan and cook the onions until brown. Add the tomatoes and turmeric and stir-fry for 4–5 minutes. Add the tamarind extract and bring to a boil, reduce the heat and simmer for a further 5 minutes. Add the coconut paste to the sauce and cook until the sauce thickens. Add the salt and curry leaves. Gently add the fried fish to the curry and simmer for 5 minutes. Garnish with curry leaves.

Ingredients

2 tbsp lemon juice

2 lb small whole fresh fish, such as sardines

Vegetable oil, for frying

5 tbsp peanut oil

1 tsp mustard seeds

½ tsp fenugreek seeds

2 cardamoms

1 cinnamon stick

2 cloves

6 whole red chillies

4 ½ oz fresh coconut, grated

1 oz tamarind, soaked in ½ cup water

½ cup onions, sliced

4 ½ oz tomatoes, skinned and chopped

1 tsp ground turmeric

Salt, to taste

10 curry leaves, plus extra for garnishing

Fish Curry

Serving suggestion

Serve hot with boiled rice.

Method

Shell and devein the prawns, then wash and pat them dry. Put the coconut in a blender or food processor with 4 tbsp water and blend to make a fine paste.

Heat the oil in a pan and heat the mustard seeds until they crackle. Add the onions and cook over a medium heat until transparent. Add the garlic and ginger pastes. Stir and cook until all the liquid has evaporated. Add the ground coriander, red chilli powder, turmeric and salt. Stir to mix. Add the tomatoes and cook until soft and pulpy, stirring occasionally. Reduce the heat to low and add the prepared coconut paste and curry leaves. Stir for 2 minutes.

Add the prawns and approximately 1 ¾ cups water. Bring to a boil, reduce the heat and simmer for about 10 minutes, stirring occasionally, until the prawns are cooked. Transfer to a bowl and garnish with ginger juliennes and fresh coriander.

Ingredients

2 lb 4 oz prawns

3 oz fresh coconut, grated

4 tbsp peanut oil

1 tsp mustard seeds

1 cup onions, chopped

4 tsp garlic paste (page 4)

2 tsp ginger paste (page 4)

2 tsp ground coriander

2 tsp red chilli powder

½ tsp ground turmeric

Salt, to taste

10 ½ oz tomatoes, skinned and chopped

10 curry leaves

Chopped fresh coriander and ginger juliennes, to garnish

Prawn Curry

Serving suggestion

Serve hot with boiled rice.

Method

Place the coconut, green chillies, onions, ginger, turmeric and fresh coriander in a blender or food processor and blend to a fine paste. Set aside.

On a hot griddle or in a heavy-based frying pan, dry-fry the fennel seeds, cinnamon, cloves, cardamoms and poppy seeds. Cool, then blend to a fine powder in a blender or food processor. Place the vegetables in a pan with just enough water to cover. Add the bay leaves and salt and bring to a boil. Boil for 15–20 minutes until the vegetables are cooked. Once the vegetables are tender and the water has evaporated, add the coconut-onion paste. Stir-fry for 2–3 minutes.

Add the ground spice mixture and clarified butter or ghee. Stir well and cook for 5 minutes, stirring.

Sprinkle with cashew nuts before serving.

Vegetable Korma

Ingredients

6 oz fresh coconut, grated

2 green chillies, chopped

2 tbsp onions, chopped

1 tsp root ginger, peeled and chopped

½ tsp ground turmeric

2 tsp fresh coriander, chopped

2 tsp fennel seeds

1 cinnamon stick

3 cloves

6 cardamoms

2 tsp poppy seeds

3 ½ oz green beans, chopped

3 ½ oz carrots, siced

3 ½ oz kohlrabi, diced

3 ½ oz peas, shelled

3 ½ oz potatoes, diced

3 ½ oz tomatoes, skinned and chopped

2 bay leaves

Salt, to taste

2 tbsp clarified butter or ghee

Whole unsalted cashew nuts, to garnish

Method

Slice the tops off the tomatoes and scoop out and discard the flesh. Set the tomato shells and tops to one side. Heat the oil in a pan and cook the onions, garlic and tomato pulp over a medium heat until the moisture is completely evaporated and the oil separates from the sauce. Add the green chillies and chopped mushrooms, stir and cook over a high heat for 10–15 minutes until the water evaporates. Add the salt, garam masala, chopped mint leaves, lemon juice, cumin and half the fresh coriander. Set aside to cool. Fill each tomato with the mushroom mixture and cover with a tomato top. Place the stuffed tomatoes

on a greased baking tray and bake at 350°F for 15–20 minutes. Meanwhile, make the sauce. Heat the oil in a pan. Cook the cardamoms, bay leaf, onions, garlic and tomatoes for 5 minutes. Add 1 ¾ cups water and salt and cook for about 30 minutes, stirring occasionally. Strain through a fine sieve. Transfer the sauce to a saucepan and bring to the boil. Remove the pan from the heat and add the cream and ground mace. To serve, pour the sauce over the baked tomatoes and sprinkle with the remaining fresh coriander before serving.

Ingredients

15 firm, round tomatoes	½ tsp ground black cumin, roasted or dry-fried
2 tbsp vegetable oil	2 tsp fresh coriander, chopped
1 oz onions, chopped	5 tsp vegetable oil
1 tbsp garlic, chopped	½ tsp cardamoms
3 ½ oz tomato pulp, fresh or canned	1 bay leaf
1 tsp green chillies, finely chopped	1 oz onions, sliced
1 lb 2 oz mushrooms, chopped	2 tsp garlic
Salt, to taste	10 ½ oz tomatoes, skinned and chopped
2 tsp garam masala (page 5)	Salt, to taste
2 tsp fresh mint leaves, chopped	4 tbsp double cream
2 tsp lemon juice	½ tsp ground mace

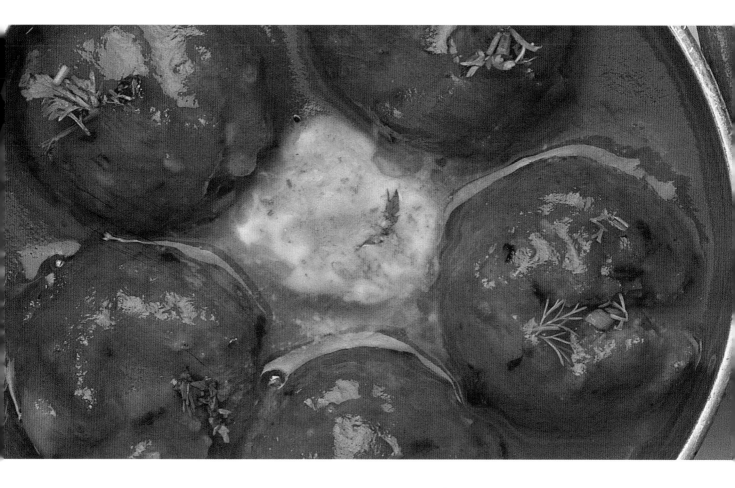

Raseele Kum-Kum

Serving suggestion

Serve on a bed of rice with a mixed side salad.

Method

Heat the oil in a pan, add the cardamoms and whole red chillies and cook over a medium heat until they begin to crackle. Add the chopped onions and cook until lightly browned. Add the turmeric, red chilli powder, white pepper and cumin and cook for 30 seconds. Cut the green pepper into long strips and add to the pan with the potatoes, carrots, button onions, cauliflower, tomatoes and button mushrooms and cook for a further 30 seconds over a high heat. Add the sugar, vinegar, garam masala and salt and cook for 30 seconds. Cover and cook for 6 minutes, stirring occasionally, until the vegetables are cooked and tender.

Garnish with green chillies, fresh coriander and green pepper rings and serve.

Subz Jalfrezi

Ingredients

5 tbsp vegetable oil

5 cardamoms

5 whole red chillies

½ cup onions, chopped

2 tsp ground turmeric

2 tsp red chilli powder

1 tsp ground white pepper

½ tsp ground cumin

1 green pepper

5 ½ oz potatoes, diced

5 ½ oz carrots, sliced

5 ½ oz button onions

5 ½ oz cauliflower, cut into small florets

5 ½ oz tomatoes, skinned and chopped

5 ½ oz button mushrooms

1 tsp sugar

2 tbsp white wine vinegar

1 tbsp garam masala (page 5)

Salt, to taste

To garnish

1 tbsp green chillies, sliced

1 tbsp fresh coriander, chopped

Green pepper, cut into rings

Serving suggestion

Serve on a bed of boiled or steamed rice.

Method

Scrape away and discard the skin of the lotus root. Cut into 1½-in long pieces, discarding the ends. Wash well under cold running water and drain.

Heat the mustard oil in a wok (kadhai) and deep-fry the pieces of lotus root for about 10 minutes until they are partly cooked. Drain and set aside.

Add ½ cup water and the lotus root to the wok and bring to the boil. Add all the spices and salt and mix in the yogurt. Cook over a medium heat until the curry thickens and the lotus root is cooked and tender, stirring frequently. Transfer to a serving dish and serve hot.

Lotus Root in Exotic Curry

Ingredients

1 lb 12 oz lotus root

9 fl oz mustard oil

2 cloves

2 green cardamoms

2 tbsp ground fennel

½ tsp ground cumin

½ tsp ground cinnamon

1 tsp ground black cardamom

1 tsp salt

3 lb 5 oz plain yogurt

Variation

Use okra in place of the lotus root.

Method

Place the green chillies, ginger and tomatoes in a blender or food processor and blend until smooth. Set aside. Heat the 4 tbsp of the clarified butter or ghee in a wok (kadhai) and brown the minced peas until the oil separates. Set aside. Heat the remaining butter or ghee in a pan and add the cumin seeds and fry for a few seconds. Add the browned pea paste, cloves, cinnamon, black pepper, ground coriander, turmeric and red chilli powder and cook for a few minutes, stirring. Stir in the green chilli, ginger and tomato purée and bring to a boil. Add the diced potatoes and cook for 10–15 minutes until the potatoes are cooked and tender. Season with salt and garam masala, garnish with fresh coriander

and serve hot.

Minced Peas and Potatoes

Ingredients

1–2 green chillies, chopped

1 ½-in piece root ginger, peeled and chopped

14 oz tomatoes, skinned and chopped

5 tbsp clarified butter or ghee

10 ½ oz peas, minced

1 tsp cumin seeds

6 cloves, ground

2 tsp ground cinnamon

1 tsp ground black pepper

1 tbsp ground coriander

1 tsp ground turmeric

½ tsp red chilli powder

5–6 small potatoes, diced

Salt, to taste

1 tbsp garam masala (page 5)

2 tbsp chopped fresh coriander, to garnish

Serving suggestion

Serve with naan or paratha.

Method

Dry-fry the coriander, cumin, poppy and sesame seeds on a hot griddle or in a heavy-based frying pan. Allow to cool, then crush. Dry-fry the coconut separately on the griddle or in the frying pan and set aside. Wash and soak the tamarind in 1 cup warm water. After 10 minutes, mash well, squeeze and discard the pulp. Set the juices aside. Slit the eggplants along about ¾ of their length. Heat the oil in a wok (kadhai) and fry the aubergines lightly. Remove from the pan and set aside. In the same oil, brown the ginger and garlic pastes, ground spices, turmeric, red chilli powder, curry leaves and coconut.

Cook gently, stirring occasionally and adding a little water if the sauce begins to burn. Add the eggplant, 2 cups water and salt and mix well. Simmer for 10 minutes. Add the tamarind juice through a sieve and simmer until the sauce thickens. Garnish with green chillies, ginger juliennes and tomato quarters and serve.

Ingredients

1 tsp coriander seeds

2 tsp cumin seeds

2 tsp poppy seeds

2 tsp sesame seeds

11/4 oz desiccated coconut

1 tbsp tamarind

14 oz baby eggplants

8 tbsp mustard oil

2 tsp ginger paste (page 4)

2 tsp garlic paste (page 4)

1 tsp ground turmeric

2 tsp red chilli powder

10 curry leaves

Salt, to taste

Slit green chillies, ginger juliennes and tomato quarters, to garnish

Curried Eggplant

Serving suggestion

Serve with plain boiled rice or Indian bread.

Method

Wash and dry the okra, then cut it into 1-in pieces.

Heat the groundnut oil in a wok (kadhai) and deep-fry the okra over a medium heat for about 5–6 minutes until crisp. Drain and reserve the oil and okra separately. Place the cashew nuts and the coconut in a blender or food processor, add the coconut milk and blend to make a fine paste. Heat 5 tbsp of the reserved oil, add the cumin and mustard seeds, lentils, whole red chillies and the curry leaves. Cook over a medium heat until the seeds begin to crackle.

Add the onions and cook until golden brown. Stir in the tomatoes, then add the red chilli powder, turmeric, coriander and salt. Cook until the fat rises to the surface, stirring continuously. Reduce the heat, add the coconut paste and cook for a further 2 minutes, stirring. Remove the pan from the heat and add the yogurt. Stir in 1 ¾ cups water. Return the pan to the heat and bring to a boil. Simmer for 15 minutes. Add the deep-fried okra and cook gently for 10 minutes. To serve, transfer to a shallow dish and garnish with the green chillies and tomato quarters.

Ingredients

l lb 12 oz okra

Groundnut oil, for deep-frying

1 tbsp cashew nuts

3 oz fresh coconut, grated

4 tbsp coconut milk

½ tsp cumin seeds

1 tsp mustard seeds

4 tsp split red lentils

3 whole red chillies

10 curry leaves

4 ½ oz onions, chopped

9 oz tomatoes, skinned and chopped

1 tsp red chilli powder

½ tsp ground turmeric

1 tbsp ground coriander

Salt, to taste

4 ½ oz plain yogurt

Slit green chillies and tomato quarters, to garnish

Fried Okra

vegetables

Variation

Use baby eggplants or baby sweetcorn in place of okra.

Method

Parboil the peas and puffed lotus seeds in boiling water for 5 minutes. Drain and set aside. Heat the oil in a pan. Add the cloves, cinnamon sticks, bay leaf and cardamoms and cook for 30 seconds. Add the chopped onions and cook until golden. Add the ginger, garlic, green chilli and cashew nut pastes and cook until the oil separates from the sauce. Add the yogurt and cook over a low heat for 5 minutes. Add the peas, lotus seeds, salt and white pepper. Cover and cook over a low heat for 5 minutes, stirring occasionally. Stir in the cream and keep hot. In a separate pan, lightly fry the ginger juliennes in the butter.

Serve garnished with lemon wedges, cucumber slices and onion rings.

Mattar Makhana Korma

Ingredients

1 lb 5 oz) peas

7 oz puffed lotus seeds

4 tbsp vegetable oil

10 cloves

3 cinnamon sticks

1 bay leaf

8 cardamoms

2 oz onions, chopped

3 tbsp ginger paste (page 4)

3 tbsp garlic paste (page 4)

2 tbsp green chilli paste (page 5)

½ cup cashew nut paste (page 5)

1 cup plain yogurt

Salt, to taste

½ tsp ground white pepper

4 tbsp double cream

2 tsp butter

Lemon wedges, cucumber slices and onion rings, to garnish

Variation

Use green beans or broad beans in place of peas.

Method

Heat the clarified butter or ghee in a pan, add half each of the grated onion, ginger and garlic pastes and fry for 4–5 minutes. Add the grated potatoes, half the red chilli powder, turmeric and garam masala. Season with half the lemon juice and salt and set aside. Boil and peel the small potatoes. Scoop out the centres and deep-fry the shells until slightly crisp. Remove from the oil and drain well. Fill each potato shell with the prepared potato filling. Cover and set aside. Heat the 3 tbsp oil in a pan over a medium heat. Add the bay leaf, cinnamon sticks, cloves, cardamoms and black cumin seeds and fry until they begin to crackle. Mix in the remaining onions and ginger and garlic pastes and stir-fry for 2–3 minutes. Add the remaining turmeric and red chilli powder and stir-fry over a medium heat for 5–6 minutes. Stir in the yogurt. Cook until the liquid evaporates, stirring frequently.

Sprinkle with the remaining garam masala and season with salt.

Arrange the stuffed potatoes in the pan. Sprinkle with the remaining lemon juice, cover and cook for 3–4 minutes over a very low heat. Serve hot garnished with ginger juliennes.

Dum Aloo Bhojpuri

Ingredients

1 tbsp clarified butter or ghee	1 lb 5 oz small, round potatoes
3 oz onions, grated	Vegetable oil, for deep-frying
2 tbsp ginger paste (page 4)	3 tbsp vegetable oil
2 tbsp garlic paste (page 4)	1 bay leaf
7 oz potatoes, boiled and grated	2 cinnamon sticks
2 tsp red chilli powder	6 cloves
1 tsp ground turmeric	6 cardamoms
2 tsp garam masala (page 9)	½ tsp black cumin seeds
1 tbsp lemon juice	5 ¼ oz plain yogurt
Salt, to taste	Ginger juliennes, to garnish

Method

To make the koftas, clean, wash and boil the spinach leaves for 4 minutes. Cool, then squeeze out as much water from the spinach as possible and finely chop. Set aside. Grind the poppy seeds and cashew nuts to a paste with a pestle and mortar or a blender. Mix together all the remaining ingredients for the koftas, except the oil, with the paste and spinach. Divide the mixture into 8 portions. Form balls by rolling each portion between the palms of your hands.

Heat the oil in a wok (kadhai) and deep-fry the balls until golden brown. Drain, set aside and keep warm. For the sauce, heat 2 tbsp oil in a wok. Add the cumin seeds and cook for 30 seconds. Add the chopped onion and cook until browned. Add the ginger, garlic and cashew nut pastes, turmeric, red chilli powder and salt and stir-fry for 2–3 minutes. Add the chopped tomatoes and stir-fry for a further 8–10 minutes. Add ½ cup water, bring to a boil and simmer for 5 minutes. Before serving, add the koftas to the sauce and simmer for 5 minutes, until heated through. To serve, pour into a serving bowl and garnish with fresh coriander and cream.

Ingredients

For the koftas

6 oz spinach

1 tbsp poppy seeds

2 tbsp unsalted cashew nuts, coarsely chopped

½ tsp ground coriander

½ tsp ground cumin

½ tsp red chilli powder

Salt, to taste

Vegetable oil, for deep-frying

For the sauce

2 tbsp vegetable oil

½ tsp cumin seeds

1 medium onion, chopped

1 tsp ginger paste (page 4)

1 tsp garlic paste (page 4)

2 tbsp cashew nut paste (page 5)

½ tsp ground turmeric

1 tsp red chilli powder

Salt, to taste

9 oz tomatoes, skinned and chopped

Chopped fresh coriander and cream, to garnish

Curried Spinach Balls

Serving suggestion

Serve with Indian bread such as naan or paratha.

Index

Baked Prawns with Pomegranate	68	Mahi Musallam	66
Bean Curry with Mint	60	Mattar Makhana Korma	90
Butter Chicken	20	Minced Peas and Potatoes	84
		Murgh Kastoori	12
Cardamom-Flavored Lamb	30	Nahari Gosht	48
Chicken Badam Pasanda	22		
Chicken Shahjahani	10	Pepper Chicken	16
Chicken Stuffed with Nuts	8	Plantain Kofta	56
Chicken with Coconut	26	Pot Cooked Chicken	6
Creamy Chicken Curry	14	Potato and Paneer	
Curried Eggplant	86	Dumplings in Curry	52
Curried Spinach Balls	94	Prawn Balchao	70
		Prawn Curry	74
Dum Aloo Bhojpuri	92		
Fish Curry	72		
Fish in Tomato Sauce	70		
Fried Chicken Curry	18	Rara Meat	32
Fried Okra	88	Raseele Kum-Kum	78
Gosht Shahi Korma	42	Saag Murgh	28
		Safed Maas	44
Kadhai Chicken	24	Shahi Paneer	62
Kadhai Paneer	58	Subz Jalfrezi	80
Kadhi	54		
Kid nu Gosht	34	Vegetable Korma	76
Kohe Awadh	46		
		White Mince	40
Lamb Mughlai	38		
Lamb Rogan Josh	36		
Lamb with Whole Spices	50		
Lotus Root in Exotic Curry	82		